A TEA PARTY
with Obâchan

BY DARLEEN RAMOS
ILLUSTRATED BY NANCY LANE

Scott Foresman
is an imprint of

Glenview, Illinois • Boston, Massachusetts • Chandler, Arizona
Upper Saddle River, New Jersey

Illustrations
Nancy Lane

Photographs

ISBN 13: 978-0-328-51413-7
ISBN 10:   0-328-51413-6

8 9 10 V0FL 16 15 14 13

"Anna, this is your obâchan," the voice on the phone said. "I'm calling to invite you and your mother for tea."

"Hi, Grandma," Anna answered. "We'd love to have tea with you!"

"Wonderful," Obâchan said. "Now, don't forget to wear your kimonos."

Anna loved having tea with her grandmother. When the day arrived, Anna put on her bright orange kimono. Her kimono was made of silk.

Anna thought about Japan, the country where her grandmother and mother were born. She hoped that someday she would be able to visit Japan.

Anna's mother helped her tie the sash so that it was snug. Obâchan said the sash was called an *obi*.

"Is the *obi* too tight?" Anna's mother asked.

"No, it's just right," Anna answered. "Mom, can we visit Japan someday?"

Anna smiled as she tucked a yellow cotton handkerchief inside her sash.

Anna's mother smiled back.

5

Anna knocked on Obâchan's door.

Obâchan was wearing a silk kimono. It was pale green with pink flowers.

"Grandma," Anna exclaimed, "you walk in such a graceful way in your kimono."

"You will learn how too. It takes time," Obâchan said.

Anna saw that the table was set for tea. But there were other things in the room Anna had never seen before.

"What are these things?" Anna asked.

"I found some items that reminded me of Japan," Obâchan said. "I wanted to show them to you, Anna."

Anna went to a drum near the table.
"What is this drum?" she asked.
"It's called a *taiko*," Obâchan answered.
"Do you want to try it?"

Anna beat on the *taiko*. It sounded deep. Then she beat faster, and the sound of the drum changed.

"You have great rhythm!" Obâchan said.

"Maybe I could play a *taiko* in Japan," Anna said. "Can we go there sometime, Mom?"

Anna's mother smiled.

Anna saw the pink flowers in a vase.

"What are these beautiful flowers?" Anna asked.

"They are cherry blossoms," Obâchan explained. "Every spring in Japan, children gather under the blossoms of the cherry trees."

"I remember! It's called the Flower Festival," Anna's mother said.

"I'm glad you remember," Obâchan said. "Now, come and sit." She walked several paces toward the table and started to pour tea. "It's time for tea," she said.

"I love learning about Japan," Anna said. "I hope that I can go there someday."

"You will, Anna," her mother said. "I will take you to Japan and show you where I grew up."

Anna smiled brightly and sipped her tea.

A Tea Ceremony

At a tea ceremony, it is a Japanese custom for the hostess to wear a kimono. The hostess serves green tea in tea bowls instead of teacups. If a meal is served, the ceremony can last up to four hours. If no meal is served, it is the custom to serve something sweet.

It is not unusual for the guests to remove their shoes inside the home. Sometimes they kneel on woven mats. Few words are spoken during the ceremony.